THE BOOK OF BOWDEN

THE BOOK OF BOWDEN

Words of Wisdom, Faith, and Motivation by and about Bobby Bowden, College Football's Most Inspirational Coach

Jim & Julie S. Bettinger
Foreword by Burt Reynolds

Dogwood Hill Books
Tallahassee, Florida

Copyright © 2001 by James G. Bettinger and Julie S. Bettinger
First paperback edition 2007; Second paperback edition 2019

All rights reserved. No part of this book may be reproduced in any form or by any electronic or mechanical means, including information storage and retrieval systems, without written permission from the publisher, except by a reviewer who may quote passages in a review.

Published by Dogwood Hill Books
Tallahassee, Florida.
www.dogwoodhillbooks.com

ISBN: 978-1-7336802-0-2

Manufactured in the United States of America. Cover photo by Phil Coale.

To our parents, Buddy and June Strauss, and Cliff and Eleanor Bettinger, for coaching us in faith and life. And to our nephew, Robby Redding, who has shown us what true courage really means.

Contents

Foreword ix
Preface xi

Adversity 1
Age 2
Ambition 7
Ann Bowden 8
Attitude 10
Career 11
Change 14
Character 16
Childhood 17
Christianity 21
Coaching 21
Competition 33
Dependability 35
Destiny 36
Discipline 38
Enthusiasm 41
Evangelism 43
Faith 44
Fame 48
Fans 49
Fatherhood 51

Father-Son Matchups 51
Fears 55
Football 55
Football in the Family 59
Gators 63
Goals 65
God 67
Golf 70
Health 71
Heisman Trophy 72
Heroism 72
Hope 73
Humility 73
Legacy 74
Life 74
Losing 77
Loyalty 77
Marriage 78
Media 80
Mentoring 81
Milestones 82
Mistakes 86
Motivation 86
Napping 87

National Championships	89	Strategy	108
People	93	Success	110
Players	93	Television	110
Prayer	95	Temptations	113
Prejudice	97	Time Line	115
Recruiting	99	Tradition	117
Retirement	100	Values	118
Rivals	103	Winning	120
Sainthood	107	Winning Traits	121
Service	107	Youth	124

Foreword

From the moment I met Bobby Bowden I knew he was more than special. I had met, at that point in my life, four presidents and numerous irreplaceable movie stars—from Spencer Tracy, John Wayne, James Stewart, and Henry Fonda, to James Cagney and Orson Welles. I knew what real charisma meant, and I certainly knew when I was or had been in the presence of greatness.

Bobby Bowden seems to possess a little piece of every extraordinary man I've ever had the pleasure and honor to know. He is, first of all, a "people person." No one he meets—and I mean no one—is ever a stranger or ever treated beneath him.

There is a glowing light from deep inside him that never goes out. No matter what the situation or pressure he has on himself, whether from others or from his own high standards, he never imposes that pressure—by action, deeds, or words—on other people.

We have all read or heard "Saint Bobby," a moniker that no person could ever live up to. But in over thirty-four years of friendship, I've never felt Bobby Bowden was judgmental, indulging me, overestimating, underestimating, or uncomfortable with me or anyone I brought to meet him.

He never has disappointed me or anyone he calls a friend, and he takes that word *friend* very seriously.

I've sat in his office with teammates who played for him forty years ago and played with him over fifty years ago. The time seemed just as precious (usually even more for him than the old friends) and never, ever rushed.

Yes, he does sound too good to be true, but if you're waiting for the other shoe to drop, forget it. For me, he is what I would hope someday to be, to have just some of that humor, his dignity, his faith, his great curiosity for and about life, and his great ability to make all of us who know him a better person because of it.

He is the big brother I never had. I'm not alone in this love for the man, just very happy and content to be a member of an ever-growing family of people whom he has touched and changed forever.

–Burt Reynolds

Preface

If you're lucky enough to find yourself in the presence of Bobby Bowden, be prepared for a lighthearted story or two and a God-centered message, with a bit of wisdom and some football strategy thrown in.

Coach Bowden has managed to win the hearts and minds of millions through his work on and off the football field.

The year 2000 marked Bobby Bowden's silver anniversary season as head football coach at Florida State University. Beginning a quarter-century earlier, Bowden resurrected a program that had won only four games in the three seasons prior to his arrival, and he transformed it into one worthy of national acclaim. His Seminoles emerged as a perennial national power in the eighties and finally won for Bowden his first national title in 1993.

Bowden has logged more than three hundred career victories and ended the 2000 season as the second-winningest active coach in major college football. His Florida State teams once played fourteen consecutive bowl games without a loss, a span that included ten consecutive victories, something no other program has ever accomplished. Bowden also is the only coach in the history of college football to have led teams to ten or more victories for thirteen straight seasons and to have had teams finish ranked fourth or higher in the final Associated Press poll for thirteen consecutive seasons.

What's his secret formula? He'll tell you a big part of it is faith and prayer. At a time when it's not only politically incorrect, but outlawed in many public places, Bowden leads his team in prayer before and after football games. A Bowden signature is his willingness and ability to shape players for life beyond the football field by teaching them life-coping skills and values.

Robert Cleckler Bowden was born November 8, 1929, in Birmingham, Alabama. His passion for the game of football took root early. It started on the roof of his childhood home in Birmingham. From that perch, he and his father could look down on the local high school's practice field. Bowden's second childhood home offered much the same opportunity, as it overlooked a college football field.

Bowden's own football career looked like it was going to be cut short by a childhood illness. In 1943, a then thirteen-year-old Bowden was bedridden while suffering from rheumatic fever. An outstanding athlete, he was suddenly subjected to a frustrating eighteen months of confinement to recuperate following a lengthy hospital stay. No matter, Bowden's father continued to fuel the boy's enthusiasm for football, and one day he brought home a football strategy board game that young Bobby played with time after time, sometimes using it to play out football games he listened to on the radio.

Bowden recovered and went on to become an outstanding football player at Woodlawn High School, then fulfilled his lifelong dream to play for the Crimson Tide. But his coveted role as a freshman quarterback at Alabama couldn't calm the rising tide of homesickness for his high school sweetheart, Ann Estock. After his first semester, he returned to Birmingham and the two youngsters married (she was sixteen, he was nineteen). Bowden transferred to Howard College (now Samford University) in Birmingham, where, at five-foot-seven and 165 pounds, he earned Little All-America quarterback honors in 1952.

Bowden received a graduate degree from Peabody College, then went on to fulfill his professional aspirations—as a football coach.

Prior to his now-legendary accomplishments at Florida State University, Bowden achieved great success in his previous coaching stops as well, putting together a 31-6 record in four seasons at Samford University (1959-1962) before moving on to forge a 42-26 mark in six years at West Virginia (1970-1975).

The father of six children and grandfather of twenty-one (at last count), Bowden has seen three of his four sons follow their dad into coaching. As of 2000, Tommy was the head coach at Clemson; Terry, who had coached at Auburn, was an ABC television sports analyst; and Jeff—Bobby's youngest son—was in his seventh season at Florida State, as a receivers coach. Oldest son, Steve, is in private business in Birmingham. Daughter Robyn Bowden Hines, eldest of the siblings, has been a school teacher, and Ginger Bowden Madden, the youngest child in the family, is a state's attorney in Florida.

While compiling the quotes for this book, we reviewed numerous videotapes of Coach Bowden on and off the field. We couldn't help but recognize the zeal he has for the game of football. His intense involvement reminded us of another man—in Coach Bowden's words, FSU football's "first hero"—Buddy Strauss. Buddy is my (Julie's) dad, who played football at Florida State in the late 1940s and now belongs to the FSU Hall of Fame.

For every quote we've put in *The Book of Bowden*, there are probably a half dozen that were left out. These come from a variety of sources—his speeches, church visits, sideline comments, press conferences, and those etched in the minds of players from those times when Bowden spoke at a critical moment in their lives. We can only hope that this work will be an inspiration to others as well as a scrapbook of sorts for anyone who cherishes one of college football's most popular and engaging legends.

A compilation like this is a team undertaking, and we actively solicited the help of many to complete the work. We'd like to thank all of those who supported us in the endeavor, including Bobby Bowden himself; Staci Wilkshire, Coach Bowden's assistant; reference librarian Connie Morris and the FSU Strozier Library Special Collections staff; Gabe

Burke and Helen Moeller of the Leon County Public Library; Ernie Stephenson of the Fellowship of Christian Athletes; Gene Deckerhoff, "the Voice of the Seminoles"; Charlie Barnes, executive director of the Seminole Boosters; Joel Padgett, also with the Seminole Boosters; Rob Wilson, FSU's sports information director; Buddy and June Strauss; attorney Mike Coppins; Phil Coale, *Tallahassee Democrat* photographer; Catherine Strauss, photographer; Francis Rentz, Advantis/St. Joe; and Heidi Tyline King, writer and friend.

A thanks, posthumously, to one of the writers who not only had the greatest access to Coach Bowden but also managed to earn his greatest respect—Bill McGrotha of the *Tallahassee Democrat*.

–Jim & Julie S. Bettinger

Their little eyes are upon you,
And they're watching you night and day.
There are little ears that quickly
Take in every word you say.

There's a wide-eyed little fellow.
Who believes you're always right;
And his ears are always open
And he watches day and night.

You're setting an example
Every day in all you do,
To the little boy who's waiting
To grow to be like you.

—Anonymous

THE BOOK OF BOWDEN

> COACH BOWDEN HAS A VERY WARM PERSONALITY, AND IS GOOD WITH PEOPLE. BUT THE MAIN THING I THINK ABOUT HIM IS THAT HE'S GOT A STRONG GOAL-ORIENTED SIDE. HE'S THE KIND OF GUY WHO'S ALWAYS GOT THE MOST OUT OF HIS ABILITY. HE HAS A STRONG WORK ETHIC, AND HE KNEW WHAT IT TOOK TO WIN. I DON'T CARE HOW GOOD YOU ARE WITH PEOPLE, IF YOU DON'T HAVE THAT WORK ETHIC, YOU WON'T SUCCEED.
> —*Wally Woodham, part of the "WallyJimmyJordham" quarterback duo at FSU 1977–1979*

ADVERSITY

Already I'd been praying to God about my sickness, but this time I prayed a special prayer. I said, "Dear God, I know that I may not be worthy of a miracle, but if You could heal me, or at least make me better, maybe even play again, then I'll use my life through athletics to serve You."

At that point, getting down on Florida State football was the most popular pastime in Florida, second only to getting down on Richard Nixon. But I believed differently. Eventually, so would everyone else.

—*after taking the FSU head-coaching job in the mid-seventies*

Some people think it's a weakness to be behind. Folks, it's not a weakness to be behind—not if you can come back and win it. One of the greatest teaching experiences you will learn in life is to be behind and then come back to win. And until that happens to you, you don't know what kind of a team you got.

Jumping into a schedule that demanded so much of us gave us the chance to get better every game, every season. And there is no way you can understate how crucial that is. There are only two ways to go into this business: You get better or you get passed up. And that applies whether you're coming off an 0-11 season or the national championship.

AGE

I don't think of myself any differently than I did when I was a young coach at South Georgia College, or at Howard College, or at West Virginia. I haven't changed any, except maybe to put on a bunch of pounds around the waistline.

I didn't think you were supposed to coach when you were seventy. People kept burning out, and I haven't burned out.

We call ourselves "the Geritol Group."

—referring to himself, Joe Paterno, and former Iowa head coach Hayden Fry

I feel sorry for people who grow old and have no hope—who just don't believe in anything. I do and it helps me keep young.

As you get to be my age, you look for new ways every year to hang on as long as you can. I'm trying to prolong my career because I love it so much.

—explaining his use of a metal tower to observe practice and a golf cart for transportation

It's too bad. He's so young.
> —responding to the announcement of the retirement in 2000 of
> BYU coach LaVell Edwards at the age of sixty-nine

If I didn't have football, I'd sleep later. I get so excited during football season. That's one thing that definitely hasn't changed.

You say to yourself, "Am I pushing this too far? Should I get out and let younger people take over?" About the time I get ready to give up, my conscience tells me, "Nah, you can still kick 'em on Saturdays."

I don't consider myself a senior citizen. But I am.

In a way I feel just like George Foreman. He's too old, what is he still fighting for? But he's still knocking them out. So let him fight.

If I had to describe how I'm different now than how I felt the first year I was head coach at West Virginia, I'd say I feel about the same. If you said how I felt about ten years ago, I'd say about the same. Now where the difference is if I'd try to run, say, a mile, I couldn't do that.

It's like they say—you put a frog in a pan of hot water he'll pop right out of it. If you put it in there when it's cold and you keep heatin' it up, you can fry it. That's kind of the way it is for me. It's just been gradual.

—describing the effects of the aging process

I'm working around seventeen-, eighteen-, and nineteen-year-olds and coaches younger than me. It helps keep you young.

Somehow, I went from being too young to being too old. Somewhere in there, I must have been just right.

AMBITION

Yes, Dick Butkus was, in my opinion, the greatest linebacker in the NFL. His greatest asset was that desire, that ambition to be the best, whatever the sacrifice. Recruiting young men to Florida State with that kind of ambition became our goal. We knew that if that could be accomplished, then winning would be only a matter of time at Florida State.

When I go after something, I go after it hard. It has always been that way. I don't know—it's in my blood.

I've always wanted to win every doggone game I've ever coached. I've never been able to enjoy what I have done because it's not over yet, and I ain't looking back.

ANN BOWDEN

We got married. I gave the justice of the peace five dollars. That left five dollars for gas to get back to Birmingham. Talk about faith.

—on eloping when he was nineteen and Ann sixteen

Heck, that night she might have led that crowd of folks out of the stadium early!

—recalling Homecoming when Southern Miss was leading, 27-10, and FSU came back in the fourth quarter to win, 30-27

I tell you, Ann ain't afraid of nothin'.

I thought Ann was a dream that first time I ever saw her. Boy, she was something! Still is.

If she has a birthday, I pay off her bills. When I have one, she starts another one.

Bobby and Ann Bowden. Married more than fifty years and going strong. (Catherine L. Strauss, photographer)

It is always a day when I can count on Ann giving me something I don't need. Another shirt. She owes me about five forgets.

ATTITUDE

I've always thought that when something bad happens to me, something good is fixin' to follow.

I think people are good before I think they are bad. Too many people, the first time they see somebody don't like 'em right away. My first reaction is I like 'em.

Our motto is, "It's not about me." In other words, you have to put yourself last in this thing. It's the team first.

> THERE IS NOT A DAY THAT GOES BY I DON'T TRY TO RELATE TO THE PLAYERS SOMETHING I LEARNED FROM HIM.
>
> *—Rick Stockstill, Clemson recruiting coordinator,*
> *FSU quarterback 1979–81*

CAREER

I didn't want to give anyone the satisfaction of knowing I was leaving with my tail between my legs.

—on leaving West Virginia following a 9-3 season (1975)
and beating N.C. State in the Peach Bowl

I remember back when I made up my mind to take the Seminoles job, I looked at some of the future games on the schedule and almost choked when I saw what we were facing down the road. I thought, "Lawh, somebody must think we're in the National Football League. Oh, well, it won't make any difference. I ain't gonna be here long anyway."

If I'm healthy and we're winning, I'll want the option to keep coaching. I don't know what else to do.

At Florida State, that (contract) means two years. I'll have to hurry.
> *—regarding his prospects of turning around a program that had won a total of four games over the three previous seasons*

I definitely intend being here that long, the Good Lord willing. I'm glad they gave me five more years. They didn't have to at my age. If you can just stay healthy, that's the name of the game. There's no reason you can't stay (successful) if you stay healthy.

I'm a southern boy who wants to be in the Deep South. I slipped on ice once too often, got bogged down in the snow one time too many. I didn't want to act anxious, but I was eager to come to Florida State.

If I could be as popular forever as I am now, I wouldn't worry about a thing. I'd have it made. But I'm fifty-two years of age (1982). How much longer can I actively coach and make my salary?

I would be pleased to stay here for as long as I can coach. If something greater came along, bigger and better, I still don't know if I'd want to leave. Matter of fact, I know I wouldn't. When you get my age you like to settle down (1981).

Before I came here, if I had to write a book about what I thought would probably happen to me, I wouldn't have written that I would be here twenty-five years. Bobby would go down to Florida State and wait for Shug Jordan and Bear Bryant to retire, and let two guys replace them, and then probably after that he would get one of those two jobs. Preferably in Alabama.

It means we are married and nobody's going to put our marriage asunder. I didn't want to go anywhere. I love it here. Florida State and its fans aren't spoiled yet.

⁓

Since I was young I have done this sort of speaking, and people would say I ought to be a real minister. But I never felt like I was called. I felt more like I was called to coaching.

⁓

As long as they want me, they got me. Yes, I would expect to be here the rest of my coaching life—if I can coach good enough.

—after negotiating his contract in 1979

⁓

CHANGE

It's hard to see the need for change when you're doing well. Changes are always easier to make when things can't get much worse.

⁓

I'm not too proud to change. I like to win too much.

CHARACTER

I learned a long time ago that you don't have to go around using bad language and fighting and trying to hurt people to show others how macho you are. That stuff won't get you anywhere. It just shows lack of vocabulary and character.

Character is so important to the type of young men we're trying to bring along. And don't confuse reputation with character. Reputation is something that's seen; character is being. Reputation is your photograph; character is your face. Reputation is something you manufacture; character is grown. Reputation is something you have when you come to town; character is what you have when you leave town. Reputation is what man says about you; character is what God knows about you.

Dependability, hard work, a boy who honors his father and mother.

—describing character

CHILDHOOD

When I was a boy, my dad used to carry me up on top of the roof where we used to sit for hours upon hours watching the Woodlawn team practice. And when they were passing and punting, running plays and such, I really became infatuated with what I was seeing out on that playing field. I didn't have the foggiest idea of what was going on, but, gee whiz, it sure looked exciting. For there was something about those rich sounds I kept hearing each afternoon—the thump of shoulder pads crashing together, the bark of the head coach, and the blare of the Colonel's fight song being pounded out by the marching band. I could hardly wait to be part of it all.

—on growing up in Birmingham in a house that overlooked Woodlawn High School's football field

Probably one of the biggest thrills that I had was when they used to practice kicking field goals. Their kicker was always pretty good and the ball used to always go sailing over the goal, across the fence and over by our chicken coop. Needless to say, it got a bit exciting for those chickens.

Football sorta became ingrained into my lifestyle while I was growing up next to those football fields. I just couldn't wait to go out and play football. Every day I'd go out early and catch passes before all of the college players got there. And if someone wanted to throw the ball, I'd go out and play catch with 'em.

—Bowden's second childhood home, near Howard College (now Samford University), overlooked the school's football field

On Sunday mornings nobody in our house got up and went out to play golf; nobody read the Sunday newspaper. We got ready for church. And there was never a vote taken.

The worst thing growing up was boiled okra. I'll eat fried okra nowadays, but I still can't stomach boiled okra. My dog got big on the boiled okra I would slip to him under the table.

I was a momma's boy.

I basically listened to a play-by-play of World War II for a year. I would imagine what every place looked like: what the terrain of the battlefield was like, what the army units looked like, and how the sounds and smells of the war must have been. I had a pretty good map in my head of where things were in Europe and I even began to learn which generals were leading which units.

—describing his activities when bedridden with rheumatic fever as a teenager

One day Dad brought home a football game on a game board for me to play. It was one of those games where it's all strategy, calling the proper plays, and matching wits with your opponent.

One day I listened to an Alabama game on the radio when they were playing Mississippi State. According to my little game, using the same plays, Alabama should have won, but they didn't.

However, by the end of the season Alabama had gotten much better. So did I.

—describing his days of rheumatic fever

Dr. Warwick said, "Bobby, your heart is as good as anybody's. The scar tissue has all healed. Go get 'em! Sic 'em!"

I remember breaking down and crying that day, right in the same room with Mother and Dr. Warwick. I just couldn't help it, for it seemed as if a tremendous burden had been lifted. No doubt about it, I was definitely the luckiest guy around. God had really blessed me.

—on recovering from rheumatic fever at age fourteen

When I was a small boy I idolized a guy named Jimmy Tarrant . . . he was an All-Stater and went on to Howard College and was a Little All-American. I remember seeing Jimmy every Sunday in our church. I thought, "Man, if he goes to church and isn't a sissy, then going to church ain't gonna make me a sissy."

CHRISTIANITY

I firmly believe it's better for a man never to have been born, than never to have been born again. When you're born again, you're born again in your soul, and you have the promise that your soul will never die. I really believe that.

―

No one knows when he or she is going to die. So, if we're going to accept Christ, we'd better not wait, because death might come in the blink of an eye.

―

I think many Christians make a mistake. If you look at all of the apostles Jesus had, you'll learn that most of 'em were pretty sorry in one way or another at one time or another. Nobody's perfect.

―

COACHING

I'm a football coach. I love the dadgum game.

―

Okay, guys, you know what needs to be done out there! (Phil Coale photo)

To me, it's like Br'er Rabbit been thrown in the briar patch—oh, what a tough way to make a living! I play the game I enjoy, and I talk about the game I enjoy.

I do not want our boys to smoke, drink, or cut classes, and I encourage church attendance. As far as coaches are concerned, I have surrounded myself with men who have religious convictions.

You are never any better than your next game. It will mean more to me later.

—referring to his two hundredth career coaching victory

The off-the-field problems have gotten so extended so much nowadays that it seems like you don't have time (for football). You have your conference call, talk show, meetings, faculty luncheons, Burger King commercials . . .

I have always gotten my greatest pleasure out of breaking down film, learning about opponents and yourself, then implementing a game plan to take advantage of your strengths and their weaknesses.

I always felt I needed to hear the boys if they needed to talk to you. It's more important than staff meetings or anything.

A coach is like an auto mechanic who has all the parts of a car laid out. If there's a piece missing, the thing won't work. You've got to find that piece.

Some coaches are just teachers. Some are mainly motivators. The best coach has a blend of both. It's hard to find those who are good at both teaching and coaching.

The similarities between leading troops in battle and coaching a team are well documented. You face similar tasks of motivation, preparation, teamwork, discipline.

―

I have an obligation to set an example . . . not by saying, "Do as I say, not as I do." Coaches must set an example in dress, language, actions.

―

Here's the evolution of an old coach. First, you don't have anything and do all your walking on the field. As you get older you move to a tower where you can see everything—and next will be the golf cart!

―

I've always felt they ought to fire the coaches who cheat. If Bobby Bowden goes out and buys a football player, fire me right now.

―

You can't afford to look back in this business until you're through. If you're still in it, you've always got that next game ahead.

I'm grading the coaches while they're grading the players. I look to see if (the coaches) are teaching the right techniques, teaching the right moves.

I won't tolerate a womanizer, I won't tolerate a drunk, and I won't tolerate a cheater. Those are the things that'll cost you your job.

—addressing assistant coaches

The times have changed. You got ACC calls, television shows, booster meetings. So there are very few coaches who call their own plays anyway. I'll bet'cha 90 or 95 percent of coaches don't call plays. A lot of people might not believe that, but I bet'cha it's true.

Football, whether people like to admit it or not, is one of those "Well-what-have-you-done-for-me-lately?" things. In other words, when you're winning, you're okay, but when you start losing, you lose your contract, and I realize that.

I still believe that winning is the greatest feeling there is in coaching, but I probably get the most satisfaction out of putting in the strategies and watching them play out.

To tell you the truth, when I started out, I never thought about breaking records or getting this many wins or that many. I just wanted to coach football and win games. So far, it's worked out okay, so I guess I'll just stick with that.

I was a senior playing in my last college game, and my coach walked in the night we were going to play. He called seven guys out and said, "You are through. You were at the fair on Thursday night."

We lost, 14-0, to a team we should have beaten to end my career. That was always in my craw. That's why I don't believe in suspensions. Punish the person who did something—take away his per diem or meals—but why punish everybody?

Somewhere along the line, I hope you've learned from my experience that you've got to run smart as well as hard. You've got to motivate your staff and your players. You've got to keep fans interested. You've got to stay on the good side of the university administrators and the boosters. And while you're doing all that, you've got to hold together a marriage and a family.

–speaking with his two oldest coaching sons

"What in the world am I doing in this profession?" I ask myself. "I don't have to put up with this. I can quit, go to Birmingham, and work in my father's real estate company. Nothing's worth this kind of abuse."

*—after his West Virginia team lost to
Pittsburgh, 36-35, in 1970 after leading, 35-8, at the half*

Coaching, in a way, has many of the same traits as evangelism. You attempt to make your point, relay your beliefs, and encourage your audience to take part in all this. Football or religion, it's much the same.

I've always felt that Darrell Mudra (Bowden's predecessor at FSU) would have won more games than I (did) my first year of '76. The players were geared to his style. You've got to recruit players to your style.

I think you can go back to a lot of coaches down through the years, and you can name some who could not communicate (on the young people's level) as well as they had—who were not interested any longer—and they would have been better off getting out.

It's awful easy to put the blame on your staff or one of the players, but I'm the head coach, I'm responsible. If we get an intercepted pass, I threw it—I'm the head coach. If we get a punt blocked, I caused it. A bad practice, a bad game—it's up to me to assume the responsibility—I'm the head coach.

Coaches steal ideas from one another all the time. There ain't any secrets in coaching.

The Book of Bowden

When you run trick plays and they work, you're a genius. But when they don't work, folks question your sanity.

When you get in a national championship game, the pressure is unbelievable. If all of us coaches had that much pressure every week for every game, we'd all be dead.

If you appease your players, the first thing you know the tail will be wagging the dog. This dog ain't gonna let that happen.

To be a coach today you must be a teacher, father, mother, psychologist, counselor, disciplinarian, and Lord-knows-what-else. If all we had to do was coach, they'd have cut our salaries because coaching is the easiest part of the job.

You boys are going to find out . . . pretty quickly, if you haven't already. Lose a game here and there, especially a big game you're expected to win, and folks will turn on you in a second.

—advice to his coaching sons

Football is not life or death to us. Football is a method of making a living to support our families. You have to win. But if you were selling insurance, you'd have to sell that. You'd still have to win.

COMPETITION

I don't believe in playing without a scoreboard. I don't feel there is any accomplishment with a tie. I think if one of my teams was playing Notre Dame for the national title and I had the choice of winning or losing or going for the tie, I would go for the win.

This is where I get my biggest thrill, looking for a flaw in the other guy's defense. It's like you're in a writing contest and you find out the other guy doesn't dot his i's. You say to yourself, I got him. I dot my i's.

I like to think I've mellowed as I've grown older, that I've learned to separate my competitive nature on the football field from the give-and-take that's healthy in the rest of my life. But one of the great things about making your living in sports is being forgiven for slipping up now and then and letting your competitive instincts show.

> BOBBY IS ONE OF THOSE GUYS WHO WANTS TO COACH AS LONG AS THERE IS BREATH IN HIM. HE HASN'T SAID IT TO ME IN THESE WORDS, BUT CLEARLY BOBBY WANTS TO GO OUT (OF COACHING) BEFORE HE NEEDS TO. HE WANTS TO GO OUT WHEN HE'S STILL DOING WELL, STILL SUCCESSFUL, AND NOT MAKING THE MISTAKE OF SOME COACHES BY STAYING TOO LONG.
>
> —attorney Richard Woods, after negotiating Bowden's lifetime contract

DEPENDABILITY

Dependability is the fulfillment of an obligation. It's also saying, "I'm going to show up on time," and then doing it. It's saying, "I'm going to play football—not chase cheerleaders." Dependability is also saying, "I'm going to do my job whatever the price."

DESTINY

All that has happened in my life has reaffirmed what I had always believed, and believe more than ever today, that God has a purpose for everyone. I believe the things that happen in a person's life are just brief stops along the highway as he or she travels to get where God wants him or her to be.

If you had said to me, "Bobby, someday you are going to be offered the head coaching job at Auburn and you're going to turn it down," I would have told you, "There's no way I'd turn that one down. You'd better get your head examined."

I would like to think I'd probably gone into the military. And I like music. I might have liked to have been a bandleader.
 —on what he might have done had he not gone on to coach football

Bobby Bowden understands all about destiny, and that it's in God's hands. (Phil Coale photo)

DISCIPLINE

So let's start with hair. I'm not going to ask you to look like Kojaks, but we are going to keep it neat and we are going to look like football players.

We're also gonna go to class and get up for breakfast. And there's not gonna be any room on this team for individuals who've got to smoke and drink. If you do then you're gonna be gone.

Next, we're gonna ask that you attend church regularly and write your mom and dad. It'll mean a lot to them and more to you over the years.

—first speech to the first FSU team

Discipline to me is sacrifice; it's willingness to give up something you want to do, so you can better yourself.

If you have a bird in your hand and squeeze it too tight, then you'll squeeze it to death. But if you don't hold it tightly enough, then it'll fly away.

—describing the fine balance of discipline

⁓

I've received no backlash from anyone on the subject of tightened discipline; you've got to remember that discipline is nothing new, it has to be a part of football.

⁓

Discipline is such an important characteristic, I think it probably is one of the most important characteristics a man can have. You simply are not gonna win in football if your team's not disciplined.

⁓

When asked if discipline was the key to winning:
If it was, Army and Navy would be playing for the national championship every year.

⁓

That's the worst thing I hate to hear—that I don't control and discipline our kids. I probably catch a lot of it because I don't tell people exactly what we've done. I've got my standards, and I've got my pride. I'm not going to let a kid get something on me.

A democracy is dependent upon disciplined people. That's the way democracy works and without it, democracy's gonna fall. Maybe through football we're helping a little bit disciplining these young men.

Football teaches the value of controlling yourself. We design offensive plays to attack defenses that are overly aggressive. We run reverses and screens that just take the heart right out of defenses that are so fired up they forget where they are on the field . . . You just ain't gonna win at anything playing out of control.

> BOBBY WAS A DEDICATED FOOTBALL MAN. WE PLAYED FOOTBALL DURING THE DAY, BUT HE PLAYED FOOTBALL IN HIS HEAD AT NIGHT. HE WAS DRIVEN.
>
> *—Dennis Hudson, childhood friend, who loaned Bowden twenty bucks to get married*

ENTHUSIASM

I believe in discipline and enthusiasm in everything you do in life, and you coach what you believe. If we can be enthusiastic in the little things we do, it will carry over to a winning season.

I'll tell you the truth, some nights I go home and I just can't wait for sleep to be over, just so I can go out and begin the next day.

Few coaches, if any, match up to Bowden when it comes to enthusiasm for the game. (Phil Coale photo)

You're asking tough questions about how much is too much, about where you draw the line between dedication and being so dadgum obsessive about your work that you start to lose touch with other parts of your life. I'm proud of you for asking those kinds of questions. When you come up with some answers, you be sure and share them with me. We'll be on to something bigger than winning football.

EVANGELISM

I reckon there will be some who will say, "Here comes another of them dadgum coaches who's gonna preach to us." Well, those folks are right in a way. I am going to talk about God and keep talking about Him whenever and wherever I have the opportunity. I'm going to preach and certainly not going to judge anyone who wants to believe differently. But as long as the words will come out of my mouth, I'm going to say what I believe to be true. And if you want to call that preaching, then so be it.

My fear for my immortal soul is that I might have done or said something—or not done or said something—and that those actions or inactions might cause one of the young men under my charge to go to hell, because I believe there is a hell just as much as I believe there's a heaven.

> HE'S LIKE A FATHER FIGURE TO US. HE'S NOT SO BIG THAT YOU CAN'T REALLY SIT DOWN AND TALK TO HIM AS A FATHER OR AS A COACH.
> —Corey Simon, FSU noseguard, 1999

FAITH

It is better to have faith in a cause that will ultimately succeed than to succeed in a cause that will ultimately fail.

To me, religion—faith—is the only real thing in life. Everything else, you're just getting through until the day you die. Faith—trust in God—should be the No. 1 priority in life.

I tell my athletes, "Men, believe me, when things seem the darkest, have faith in Jesus. No matter how impossible things look, don't ever give up."

You want to know what a real test of faith is? That's when you go to church and reach into your pocket and all you got is a twenty-dollar bill.

The older I get, the more confident I've become in the faith I acquired as a child in my parents' home and carried with me all these years. I trust in God's will, even when I don't know what ends are being served.

I can't tell you how many times I've stood at what I thought was a dead end to discover that a door was about to open to a new path, that a new opportunity was about to present itself. If I just believed and trusted enough in Him, the meaning became clear.

I don't know what God's voice sounds like, but I think He's talked to me a couple of times. I may not be very smart, but I'm smart enough to know that His power intervened in my life.

You may have to pay a price for what you've done, but it doesn't mean you're a failure. You can get beyond it if you have faith.

–from a letter he sent to a player who was incarcerated for drugs

I've seen people change their lives around, becoming entirely new human beings through faith. I call that a miracle, and it's the only proof I need of God working in our lives.

I'm a firm believer in God and country and Florida State football.

I think God made it simple. Just accept Him and believe.

FAME

I was running out of gas on I-10, and pulled off at night and finally found this little station that was open. This fellow came out. He kept looking me over. Finally, he said: "I know you—you're the fellow that sells them Fords on TV."

As far as being some sort of dadgum coaching legend, I find that kind of ridiculous. I know this—if being driven to succeed makes a person (into someone) some other folks might look up to, then I might be that kind of a person.

Joe Smith, college student, can get arrested for drunk driving or for getting in a fight, and the story ain't going to be on ESPN or in the sports pages the next morning. No one is going to be insisting the university kick him out. But the rules are different for our coaches and kids. It's part of what changes when you have great success and everybody seems to know who you are.

Well, they're pickin' us No. 1 to start the season. That's the good news. The bad news is that the same people picked us No. 1 in 1988. That was the year we stayed in contention all the way until the kickoff of the first game.
—*Miami beat FSU, 31-0, in that 1988 opener*

FANS

After losing to Florida the way we did last year, it might not be a good idea for me to get out on a boat with some of our alumni.
—*on deciding to go golfing with alumni instead of fishing*

We're better than I expected, but not as good as our alumni think.

FATHERHOOD

Like most fathers, I can sometimes talk about what's deepest in my heart to strangers more easily than to my own children.

FATHER-SON MATCHUPS

If we win, it's a dream come true. If we don't, it's a nightmare. And I ain't shaking his hand after the game, either.

—regarding the first "father-son coaching matchup" in major college football, Terry Bowden vs. Bobby Bowden in 1999, when FSU beat Tommy's Clemson team for Dad's three hundredth coaching victory

I can probably anticipate some of the things he (Tommy) is going to do. But he will also be able to anticipate some of the things I would do. My advantage is I have someone else calling plays. But he will have a sneaking idea if we are going to run a reverse. I will guarantee you. I've been able to watch Terry's games and Tommy's on television and sometimes predict, here comes a reverse.

We might have a trick or two up our sleeve. I'm going to have one for him, now. And I know he's going to have one for me.

I don't think I will have any different feeling. I will go up and look at the film, and I will get scared like I always do. I will wonder, "How in the world are we going to beat this team?" like I would do if we were playing Leon (High School). Then as the week progresses, you begin to see things you think might go. Then you get to feeling a little better. They will probably do the same thing.

This game (FSU-Clemson) has nearly got the magnitude of when we play Florida and when we play Miami. I have that feeling. I have that "something special" feeling.

They'll probably be afraid to express it. They may whisper it to Tommy—"Hey, Tommy, we're really for you"—but they know I got the will. They can't let me know 'cause I can take them out of that will.

Bobby and son, Jeff, enjoy a lighter moment in 1999 on the FSU sideline. (Phil Coale photo)

The Book of Bowden

I'm sure there will be sympathy both ways. Some won't want the old man to lose; others might want the son to get a break.

I'm not concerned. Ann likes spending too much for me to lose that game.

Mama's happy, I know that. Mama wanted a close game where I'd win because I'm older and I've got more riding on it and where her boy would look good. I thought he looked good.

We still call each other. The main thing, we won't discuss X's and O's. Can't do that now. We used to could help each other a lot. We've always been able to pass that information around. Can't do that anymore.

—referring to Tommy Bowden

FEARS

The good Lord might not want to take me, but He might be after the pilot.

—on his fear of small planes

FOOTBALL

First of all, we've got to have a basic understanding of who's in charge around here. There can never be a question of that.

Well, I am the new guy around here. I'm the head coach. And in the past three years *your* Florida State football team has managed to win only four games and in the meantime lose twenty-nine. Y'all have tried it your way, and where did it get you? Nowhere. Now, I think I know how to win. And from now on at Florida State we're gonna do things my way. If you don't like it, then hit the door. Go somewhere else. Because if winning doesn't mean something to you then we don't need you. From now on, it's going to be an honor to wear a garnet jersey and represent Florida State University. We're gonna win again at Florida State.

The Book of Bowden

No matter what happens on the field today, I want you to have fun when you're in there—enjoy yourselves. If you get knocked down, get up. I know you're ready to play—just keep your pride and confidence on the field and play with class. But also remember that those sixty minutes on the field may help determine the rest of your life.

—pre-game, FSU vs. LSU, October 1979

I'm inclined to believe there are too many reformers in the American public. The biggest task that the government has today is to reform the reformers. These people infer that anybody either directly or indirectly interested in football is more or less crazy and unable to see the light because his eyes are blurred with floating specks of pigskin. I'm not inclined to believe that there are over two hundred thirty million lunatics in this country.

A stronger opponent can't hurt you if he can't catch you. There ain't no substitute for speed.

I love taking a group of young men in the late summer and molding them into a team.

Man, I can't imagine a high greater than the feeling of standing on the sidelines during an exciting game with sixty to seventy thousand people in the stands. I get goose bumps just thinking about it.

You can take all the X's and the O's and the fancy formations and the hidden defenses, but if you don't block and tackle better than the people you're playing, you'll lose.

If dancing and pointing fingers when they're excited about playing football is the worst thing they do, I reckon we can forgive them.

—referring to show-off behavior

The good news is that our defense is giving up only one touchdown a game. The bad news is that our offense is doing the same.

FOOTBALL IN THE FAMILY

Out of all my kids, Tommy was the most disciplined. The best kid. If you said, be in at eight o'clock, he was in at eight o'clock. Terry Bowden, now, would come in when he got good and ready.

I would say, "Terry, I'm gonna whip you." And he would say, "Hurry up and get it over with, because I'm getting ready to head out again."

If there's one thing that connects all of us, it's that trait—dogged perseverance. When all else fails, we work hard.

—referring to shared family traits

There are things that happen that make you leery of your children going into your profession. But it happens in all professions.

When y'all started talking about coaching, my attitude was, "Boys, if you feel that the only way you're going to be happy is if you're coaching I want you to do it. But if you think you'd be just as happy in law or medicine or banking, I kinda hope you go that way. At least then we wouldn't be competing against one another."

I did not encourage my sons to go into coaching. I discouraged them. I didn't want them in there competing against me.

All of you have watched me enough to know about highs and lows. Still, as a father, I can't help worrying. There's enough pressure already in this business without adding in the problem of competing against your own family.

I know their mother—she'd give them all my plays.
—explaining why he didn't want to play against his sons' teams

I figured I could have handled the criticism from fans who thought I was favoring my own kids, but I thought if I brought you in immediately you might not have been accepted by the team. "There goes Daddy's boy," they'd say.

—his reasoning for not giving his son, Tommy, a football scholarship

---

I never cut them a break. Right or wrong, I thought they'd have a greater sense of accomplishment if they knew they had done it on their own.

—about how he treated his sons as
football players and assistant coaches

When I look back on those times, I feel like those were some of the luckiest years of my life. To have my sons out there on the football field with me, for us to be doing something that meant so much to all of us—to be at the family business—boy, that was something special. What we're doing now is about as close as we can get to what we were doing then. We're still playing the game as a family.

I think y'all have to be careful about measuring yourself against some image you or others have created. You'll always fall short. And you'll always be punishing yourself. There's only one person who's ever been perfect on this earth, and He ain't your Daddy.

–talking to his kids about being in their father's shadow

I had to listen to Ann: "You play everybody else's son, but you won't put your own boy on the schedule to help him out!"

–on putting Auburn on the schedule when his son, Terry, was head coach there

---

THE AMOUNT OF VICTORIES, EVEN THOUGH AN AMAZING FEAT, STILL DOESN'T DESCRIBE ALL COACH BOWDEN HAS ACCOMPLISHED AT FLORIDA STATE. I DON'T RECOGNIZE HIM FROM THE TOMAHAWK THAT LIES ON THE HELMETS OF HIS PLAYERS, BUT I RESPECT HIM AS THE MAN OF GOD THAT HE IS.

–Deion Sanders, FSU defensive back 1985–1988

GATORS

I know a lot of you look at me and ask if this is a big-time coach. I don't know what a big-time coach is. But I know if I beat Florida, I'll be a big-time coach.

–first FSU press conference, 1976

It ain't turned around until we beat the Gators.

–after winning five games his first season at FSU

Our fans just plain don't like to lose to them Gators, and they don't cotton much to coaches who do. I wasn't too happy about it either. I don't like losing to anybody six times in a row, not even in Ping-Pong.

–following six straight losses to the Gators, 1981 through 1986

The hardest thing about this whole thing was breaking the drought. The six-straight thing was a psychological strain– whatever you want to call it. I can't explain it.

–on finally beating the Gators after six consecutive losses. The Seminoles finished the regular season 11-0.

Well, he ain't gonna play, is he?
> —responding to a reporter's question, "What are you going to do about Spurrier?" In the first meeting between the two coaches, FSU beat the Gators, 45-30, in 1990.

The game is over. This is not about a football game. I've never let the Florida State-Gator thing really affect my life.
> —responding to questions about having back surgery in Gainesville

Steve (Spurrier) has an innovative mind, which I like . . . He's dadgum clever.

When I am around Steve (Spurrier), I enjoy him and he puts up with me. We get along fine. I really admire the job he has done. I have the utmost respect for him because he has beaten me so many times.

I feel mighty humble. I appreciate this win. I ain't gonna brag too much.

—on beating the Gators in 1987

Either way it was a great win—I mean tie.
—post-game interview in 1994, after FSU trailed Florida, 31-3, and came back in the fourth quarter to forge a 31-31 tie at the end

GOALS

Little did I know back then, while I was growing up in that white frame house behind the Woodlawn football stadium, that someday I would become a head coach at a major university like Florida State. But I did. And to me, that has to be a great example of what young people all over this country are striving for—to reach the American Dream.

Men, we have never had a perfect season here at Florida State. If you will do everything we ask, it will happen. Trust me.

—what he told the team when they set and reached their goal of having an undefeated season in 1999

I want to win every game and have the best football team in the United States. I want to have a perfect season. We came close the last two years but they weren't perfect. If I ever accomplish that, I'll set a higher goal and go after that. I'd like to play a perfect game of golf.

—stated in 1981

Three hundred sneaks up on you. If you were young and just entered coaching, you would set goals. My goal would not be to win three hundred games. It wouldn't be to win 324. They are out of reach. There's no way I would be able to do that. You don't ever think about it.

GOD

I am living proof that it doesn't matter where you come from, or how big or little you are, if you turn your life over to God, He will do unbelievable things. And if y'all don't believe that, well, here I stand.

We are all seeking the same thing.
—on his practice of speaking to different churches and denominations

I'm giving 10 percent of my salary to God, no matter how great the sacrifice.

God is an integral part of my life. I look to God for guidance but firmly believe God helps those who help themselves. Man must help himself, but also seek guidance.

I want to be on God's squad—He's my kind of head coach.

I kind of feel, too, that none of us wants justice from God. What we want is mercy because if we got justice, we'd all go to hell. There's no way we can earn it. We aren't good enough, and can never be good enough.

The number-one thing to me is that all people are born with an innate hunger for God, and their lives are spent trying to fill this hunger. Some search for it all their life. Some don't know how to find it.

GOLF

I don't fish, I don't hunt, and I don't chase women. Golf is one recreational outlet I have.

I'd play fifty-four (holes of golf) every day if I could find the time. I really would. It gives me a chance to compete. I love to compete. I don't have to have an opponent. I can compete by myself for a low score and have a great time. I even love to practice golf.

–after playing 108 holes of golf in four days while on a speaking tour in north Florida

Sometimes I feel like if I don't play (golf), I'm gonna explode. Sometimes I get it up to here with the ringing telephone, all the details. It's like steam. Gotta come out, and it's my way of letting it off . . . Now, come August, I put away my clubs and I won't touch 'em again until after recruiting, in February. Football, in season, consumes me.

> ANYBODY THAT HAS LASTED AS LONG AS HE HAS, HAS TO BE DOING THINGS THE RIGHT WAY. YOU HAVE TO BE A GOOD PERSON, AND YOU HAVE TO GET ALONG WITH PEOPLE. THAT'S WHAT WE HAVE TO SAY WE ADMIRE ABOUT COACH BOBBY BOWDEN: HIS ABILITY TO DO IT YEAR AFTER YEAR AFTER YEAR. THE VICTORIES HAVE ADDED UP.
>
> —*Steve Spurrier, University of Florida head football coach*

HEALTH

Normally, I don't take an aspirin or any medicine—I just will not take pills. I just feel like you should save all that for the day you need it. My last physical was two years ago, and everything was okay. I pray a lot.

–1981

If you can just stay healthy, that's the name of the game. There's no reason you can't stay (successful) if you stay healthy.

–1999

HEISMAN TROPHY

I've always been envious of coaches and schools who had a Heisman winner. It's not quite as important to the university and players as a national championship, but it has to be up there, way up there.

He has all the qualities that stand for the Heisman. To me, the Heisman Trophy winner is someone who is special, someone who is not only an outstanding athlete but an outstanding leader. That's Charlie (Ward).

HEROISM

I've been a hero before, and I've been a goat before. I have to admit, I like hero a lot better.

Kids look up to athletes. Whether we want to admit it or not, we're all hero worshippers. We don't have cowboys anymore. We don't have war heroes to admire. So most of the heroes today are athletes.

HOPE

When I have a kid who gets in trouble, I try to leave him some thread of hope. If we're so big on using football to teach the lessons of life, don't we have to offer these kids hope that there's a way to fight their way back after they stumble and fall?

HUMILITY

You've got to learn to walk away from this kind of thing. You've got to back off, son. I don't care how tough you are or how strong you are, all a little ol' 120-pound guy has to do is pull out a gun and pull the trigger, and you're nobody.

—recommendation to William Floyd, fullback on 1993 championship team

---

I'M NOT SURE WHAT A LEGEND IS, BUT I KIND OF HAVE A HUNCH THAT BOBBY IS ONE OF THOSE MEN WHO HAS ALL THE INGREDIENTS TO BE ONE. THE TRUTH IS THAT LEGENDS DON'T UNDERSTAND THEIR FOOTPRINTS. I KNOW BOBBY BOWDEN DOESN'T UNDERSTAND HIS.

—Ken Smith, team chaplain 1979–1987

LEGACY

When I leave Florida State—about a hundred years from now—I'd prefer to be remembered most for building character in young men than winning the national championship.

LIFE

Life isn't fair, because if it were, God would strike me dead where I stand, and no innocent baby would ever die.

I've been asked what the future holds for Bobby Bowden. I don't know that. I don't want to know. I think if I knew, it would ruin my life. Life is an adventure; I wouldn't want to know what's going to happen next.

I believe God has a plan for my life. And it has nothing to do with coaching and winning football games and championships and making a lot of money.

Face life now.

Don't go to your grave with a life unused.

LOSING

I hurt so bad I couldn't stand it. Every time I woke up, it was like I had been shot.

> *—following back-to-back, one-point losses in 1980 to Miami, 10-9, and then to Oklahoma, 18-17, in the Orange Bowl*

There's this debate among coaches about what motivates you more, the determination to win or the fear of losing . . . I say, I've got to win because I'm so afraid of losing. I hate that feeling of losing so much I'll do just about anything to escape it.

Sure losses hurt. But football isn't life or death.

LOYALTY

I tell my coaches, when they look at my list of requirements every year, the first thing I've got is loyalty. We're gonna be loyal to each other—I'm gonna defend you, you're gonna have to defend me. It starts there with loyalty.

> HE ALREADY HAS EVERYTHING HE NEEDS. INCLUDING ME.
>
> *—Bowden's wife, Ann, referring to her husband's Christmas presents*

MARRIAGE

I don't care when you get married, what era you live in, there's nothing easy about marriage. You've got to work at it. It truly is work.

I don't believe God wants us to divorce. But if we do, I don't believe he turns away from us either. Everything I understand about the Bible suggests He will pardon us for our mistakes. And I think He wants us to pardon ourselves, too—provided we learn from our experience and avoid making the same mistakes again.

Bobby and Ann Bowden flanked by their six children. From left to right: Steve, Terry, Ginger, Bobby, Ann, Robyn, Jeff, and Tommy. (Catherine L. Strauss, photographer)

It is a fact that when (Ann) and I were coming up people just didn't divorce as often. There was a stigma to it. And there's no doubt there's an advantage in that. If you don't consider divorce an alternative, you pretty much have to work things out.

MEDIA

The guys in the media have jobs to do; I've always understood that. They're trying to earn a living, just like me.

We are in the selling business. We need the press. I don't agree with everything they write, but a guy walks in here and I nearly feel like I owe him a story. He doesn't owe me.

Man, there's no pressure, there's none. I've not lost a game yet . . . I'm undefeated! I'll go all the way to September without losing a single ball game, y'see? But, when we play that first ball game, or when we lose that first ball game, the honeymoon with the media, well, it ends.

–1976

MENTORING

I think it's because of those men (All-American players) that I go out every Sunday and speak at different churches and speak to all kinds of youth groups. It's because back in 1947 one man came to my church and spoke to my heart, and stirred something inside me.

I am happiest when I'm in front of an audience, particularly an audience of young people telling them about the love of God.

I don't preach. I'm not qualified to preach. I like to share my experiences with God, though, especially with young people.

I go out and talk to kids because they can still be influenced. So many of them are at a crossroad in their lives. The right word at the right time might turn them in the right direction, might change them, and might steer them on to productive, happy, Christian lives.

I feel as a believer I must try as hard as I can to give them God's word, because if they don't get that, they might get the wrong word. Too many kids have already gotten the wrong word and that saddens me.

I deal with so many youngsters who have never been taught the right things to do or the right way to live. I can sell most kids on life. I can sell them on dying. But when I say, "Then comes the judgment," man, that gets their attention.

MILESTONES

When I got back to Morgantown (West Virginia) after being interviewed for this job, it was snowing and the roads were iced up and all I could think about was Florida. Then I got out of the car and slipped and fell on a sheet of ice, and I knew then what my decision was going to be.

That win got me the Florida State job.

—*on West Virginia's beating Pitt, 17-14, in 1975*

It didn't seem that great a win to me and you'd think, "Well, boy, that's got to be one of your great all times." It wasn't—for one reason. I didn't know the impact of that game and what it meant to us. I had to lose to them later on to realize how important that game was to us. It was a great win for Florida State.

—on FSU beating the Gators in 1977

Last year we managed to get this program turned around, but now those winning efforts must continue. Just because we won last year doesn't mean that it's going to happen again. Eleven other college teams—those on our schedule—have different ideas about that.

Referring to FSU's 24-19 victory over LSU in 1979:

That was the one that decided I would stay. If we had lost the game, I think I would have gone to LSU. At that time we didn't know what we could do here. We just didn't know if we could ever build this thing up. At LSU, it was a gold mine, I thought. Paul Dietzel had told me, "It's your job if you want it." I came back after that game and wrote him to take me out of it.

I still think that might be the best team we've ever beaten here.

—when FSU beat Pitt, 36-22, in Tallahassee in 1980

Most powerful Florida State team ever, yes, the best. More weapons, more depth, more togetherness. I was amazed at the togetherness of this team.

—referring to his 1987 Seminoles team that went on to defeat Nebraska, 31-28, in the Fiesta Bowl

It's going to be nice that people won't remind me every day that we never won a national championship. You know, "He can't win one, he can't win the big one."

—on beating Nebraska, 18-16, in the 1994 Orange Bowl to capture the national title

To be a national champion in both polls is really surprising to me and I'm thankful. It's very hard to be picked preseason No. 1 and then do it.

Used to be the other schools would bring it up when they recruited against us. Other coaches would say, "Look how Little League that is, look how Little League they are—you don't want to play in that thing." They don't say that anymore. They can't say that anymore. I think we can be the ones to bring up the stadium issue now.

—commenting on FSU's new stadium and university center, nicknamed "the House that Bobby Built"

I have a funny feeling that this thing is all going to come out right. We still have one weekend of football left. The right team, whoever deserves it, is going to win the national championship.

—quoted on New Year's Eve prior to beating Nebraska in the 1994 Orange Bowl

It's just nearly too good to be true. We're going to play in the big one.

—after second-ranked FSU beat top-ranked Florida, 24-21, and headed to the Sugar Bowl in 1996

If I go to my grave and I am fifth, I will be a little unhappy. Of course, the death ain't going to make me happy, either.

—on being the fifth-most-winningest coach

I know the fans want to make a big deal out of twenty years, but that really does not mean that much to me. I tell you what—I'll let everyone blow it out for my twenty-fifth year. That'll be something! I would really like to spend a quarter of a century here—if they'll have me.

MISTAKES

The greatest mistake is to continue to practice a mistake.

MOTIVATION

Fear is a motivator. It's sure motivated me through the years. I think fear of losing motivated some of our players to that national title (in 1993).

If you put two teams on the field on any given day—one with great physical ability and the other with less physical ability but great motivation—the team with the greater physical ability will win almost every time. But if you have two teams equally matched in ability, that's when the hard work, discipline, and motivation can make the difference.

> GATOR FANS HAVE TRIED THEIR HARDEST TO HATE BOWDEN . . . BUT IT HAS BECOME AN IMPOSSIBLE TASK . . . GETTING WHIPPED BY BOWDEN IS LIKE GETTING BEAT BY UNCLE MORTY IN A GAME OF CHECKERS. MORTY TALKS YOUR EAR OFF, TELLS YOU A FEW JOKES, GIVES YOU A WINK, AND TRIPLE JUMPS YOU TO WIN THE GAME.
>
> –Mike Bianchi, Gainesville Sun *sports columnist*

NAPPING

That's something I didn't used to do, taking an hour nap. I've been doing that about four or five years. It saves me.

I guess I could get burned out, but I don't think I ever will. I think I'm too lazy for that to happen. I'll go somewhere and take me a nap before I'll let myself get burned out. I've always been able to sleep and rest, and when I wake up, I'm ready to go again.

Nobody can sleep as good traveling on a plane or in a car as I can.

I can really see the value of (napping) now. If I don't do that, I'll be okay during practice. But as soon as I go home, wherever I am, I'm asleep.

NATIONAL CHAMPIONSHIPS

The main thing and the hardest thing is to get there. When you get there, you hope you can win the doggone game. But you must realize that every time you get to a national championship game, you're playing the best in the country. I don't apologize for losing to the best in the country, you know?

The plain truth is, I am not going to sell my soul to win a national championship. Bobby Bowden ain't selling his soul for nothin'.

One of the longest moments of my life . . . the referee tells me that there's one second put back on the clock after we thought time expired.

–celebrating the 1993 national championship after Nebraska attempted what would have been a winning field goal–and missed

Getting doused has become part of Bowden's championship legacy at Florida State. (Phil Coale photo)

I won't be able to savor this one until recruiting season is over. Right now, for me the most exciting thing is we won the game. I don't think, "Oh, boy, we won a national championship." That just don't ring a bell.

After getting so close for the previous six years, I was beginning to wonder if I would ever get to come here, after forty-one years of coaching, which means if that rate keeps up, I'll be 106 the next time we get to come here.
—regarding FSU's White House visit after winning the 1993 national title

I like to win it and I'm disappointed when we don't, but I came from the other side of the tracks so I'm just happy to be here.

That just shows how hard it is to win a national championship. There are just too many variables that you can't control—injury, off-the-field problems, things that can eliminate people. I'd think that if we didn't get anybody hurt, we have as good a chance as anybody else. But we might get all the bad breaks this year.

Considering that the Lord might not have allowed my winning the national title for many years, I thought, "I can accept that." But I felt like adding, "Lord, if it's not in your plan, then why do you keep letting me get so dadgum close?"

> THE MAN'S JUST A GREAT COACH, YOU KNOW. JUST AN EXCELLENT ALL-AROUND HUMAN BEING. ANYTHING HE CAN DO TO MAKE YOU BETTER AS AN ATHLETE, HE'LL DO. AND AS A BETTER PERSON, HE'LL DO. HE'S JUST A SUPER MAN.
>
> —Ron Simmons, FSU linebacker, 1977–1980

PEOPLE

Many men claim they were the reason I came to Tallahassee, but there was only one man—that man was John Bridgers.

—note to John Bridgers, former FSU athletic director, who hired Bowden to coach the Seminoles

PLAYERS

I ain't used to sending in the play, and then having the quarterback wave me off!

—explaining 1981–83 quarterback Kelly Lowery's independent spirit

The Book of Bowden

I wish we could claim that Charlie (Ward) learned how to be Charlie at Florida State. But he came to us that way. He's the son of a coach and a teacher. By high school, Charlie had already learned what sports can teach you about patience and determination.

I think basketball would be his first love simply because he can live longer.

—on why he would recommend Charlie Ward
play basketball over football

He doesn't know the meaning of the word *fear*. In fact, I just saw his grades, and he doesn't know the meaning of a lot of words.

—referring to Reggie Herring, linebacker 1978–80

I told our team before the game, "Great ballplayers make great plays." We have one great ballplayer tonight, Peter Warrick. And he made a great play. We need about five of them.

—*referring to when FSU beat Louisiana Tech, 41-7, in 1999*

PRAYER

We always pray before a game. I never pray for victory; I just pray that they do their best and ask God to take care of our players. God isn't going to win a football game for you; He's got much bigger things on his mind.

Ever since I can't remember, I've prayed. My parents taught me to pray early. I read my Bible. I've been dependent on God all my life, and I am dependent on Him now.

I've always asked for good health, wisdom, and help me to try to be good. I definitely believe in prayer.

The power of prayer at work. (Phil Coale photo)

PREJUDICE

If I could wipe out one thing in this world I think it would be racial prejudice.

I remember recruiting black players when I was a coach at West Virginia. There were always some old alums who wanted to know how many I was going to let on the team. They had a quota in their heads. Well, I tell you, you keep winning games and those old guys get color-blind pretty quick, and those quotas get stuck in their pockets.

How can folks in their right minds think that God is going to let them into heaven just because they are white and then turn away good people just because they are black? The folks who believe that are wrong, and need to go back and read their Bibles again.

There is so much prejudice and hate in the world. I don't know if man will ever get past that. It just shows how far we've gotten away from the basics of what God wanted for man. All we can do is hope and pray for understanding, tolerance, and guidance.

Racial bigotry is nothing but pure ignorance, not to mention hate; and if my vocabulary was bigger, I could probably come up with some better words to describe it.

> YOU'LL HEAR SOME SAY (ABOUT MOST COACHES), "HE CAN COACH BUT HE CAN'T RECRUIT," OR "HE CAN RECRUIT BUT CAN'T COACH." HE (BOWDEN) HAS BEEN ABLE TO MAINTAIN THE LEVEL OF GREAT PLAYERS. HE CAN RECRUIT THEM. AND ONCE HE GETS THEM, HE KNOWS HOW TO UTILIZE THEM AND KEEP THEM HAPPY. THAT'S HARD TO DO.
>
> —Mack Brown, Texas head coach who has lost more games to Bowden than anyone

RECRUITING

It means we can look a high school football player right in the eye and say, "Come to FSU. We aren't second-rate anymore."

—after beating Florida, 37-9, in 1977

Our coaches look for three main things: 1) physical ability; 2) academic potential; and 3) character. No matter how great their athletic ability, we won't take them if they lack both of the other qualities. If they lack only one, we might take a chance.

Boys and girls as they are growing up become interested in, or fans of, certain schools because of athletics. It's a shame that it is that way, but the *Tallahassee Democrat* or Associated Press is not going to pick up test scores that were made in the English department. But they will carry scores of a ball team and it flaunts that school's name in the paper. It's a help at selling the university.

RETIREMENT

I'm sure there will come a day when they will say, "You've had it, you've run your course, you are through." And when that day comes, I will have to see if there is another coaching situation to which I can contribute. If not, I will consider retirement. I am not one of those looking forward to the day I retire.

When I can't talk to kids, I'll get out.

After the game, the writers asked me, "Are you going to retire, now that you've finally won that championship?" My answer was, "Retire? Heck no. Now that I've got one, I want two. Next season I want you writers saying, 'Did you know that Bobby Bowden is the oldest football coach who ain't never won two national championships?' "

⌒

I don't know (when I'll retire). I do know that after you retire there ain't but one big event left. So I ain't in no hurry about retiring.

⌒

I have no desire to retire. I love this too much. I know I'm seventy and surely I should be saying, "It's time to get out. But really, the thought has never crossed my mind. I want to do this as long as I can."

⌒

I'd be picking weeds out of my wife's garden. That's what Ann would have me doing if I wasn't coaching.

⌒

The Bear always said, "If I retire, I'll be dead a week later." Well, he died a month later. Me? I'd just as soon die right out there on the field.

I know I can't coach forever. And I know when I do have to hang it up that I'll probably go through withdrawal—whatever that is—but I'll handle it. The Lord will take care of me and see me through it. He has never turned His back on me yet.

RIVALS

My thrill today was not beating Florida, but finishing unbeaten. Charley Pell and his staff did a good coaching job on us. They did a better job than we did, I'd have to say.

—on FSU beating Florida, 27-16, in November 1979

One of my most frustrating things in my life is to go to Auburn and get beat.

I'm gonna tell my kids there are just sixty thousand up there. They won't have time to count.
  —referring to the 105,000 screaming Michigan fans for a 1991 game

We weren't very smart at the end there. But I guess it must have been our time. That's all I can think, because Nebraska played as well or better than we did.
  —on FSU's winning its first national championship with a 1994 Orange Bowl victory over the Cornhuskers

I remember playing Tom (Osborne) in 1993. Me and him were the oldest coaches to have never won a national championship. We were fixin' to play each other and one of us was fixin' to get one of them. Well, we got it and I felt so sorry for Tom. But I don't feel sorry for him anymore, because he won three out of the next four years.
  —before Tom Osborne retired in 1997

I have never seen people with more class than I saw at Nebraska. The Nebraska fans, players, cheerleaders, band, officials, coaches, etc., gave me living testimony of what college football should be about.

He was in ways a lot like me, and the programs were similar. You had two programs taken over from the bottom, both fighting to be number one. We both had fun, and it was a fun rivalry. And you felt if you ever beat him, you had beaten one of the best in the country.

—*on coaching against Howard Schnellenberger during the latter's Miami days*

They look so good to me. I'm amazed they're not on strike.

—*on playing the University of Miami while an NFL strike was in progress*

We like to play in the Orange Bowl, but I like it better when it is someone other than Miami.

> HAIL ST. BOWDEN.
>
> *—bumper sticker circa 1978*

SAINTHOOD

You've got to be careful about that saint stuff. They put that halo over your head, and pretty soon it slips down a few inches and becomes a noose.

―

The folks who started calling me Saint Bobby were the ones who put a little twist in their voice when they said it. I think they were mostly Gator fans. But they definitely did not intend for it to be complimentary.

―

SERVICE

I've always believed in God, the Bible, and Jesus Christ. The talents God's given you should be used for His glory.

I've really been lucky because God lets me support my family. He lets me make a living through coaching the game I love, football, but I still know that the primary responsibility in my life is trying to serve God through football.

And in nearly thirty years of coaching, I've learned a big fact of life. It is that God doesn't want your ability. Instead, He wants your availability. He needs people who'll say, "God, here I am. I'm making myself available to You. What do You want me to do?"

STRATEGY

Well, I got to thinking for awhile, trying to figure out what would turn this program around. I knew that we would need a cause that people would fight for and would be willing to lay it on the line, day-in and day-out, for four years of their life . . . then it finally came . . . Beating that other school down in Gainesville just had to become our rallying point. More than that, it had to become an obsession, something our people would live and die for.

–first year of coaching at FSU, 1976

One of my biggest displeasures (is shaving). Sometimes I do it before I go to bed so I won't have to do it in the morning. That way I feel like I'm ahead of the game.

Let's win with our talent.
—*before meeting Nebraska in the 1994 Orange Bowl*

I like the idea that we're a wild offensive football team because it sells tickets, you know. But really, anybody that doesn't think we play pretty sound football, they're thinking just like I want 'em to think when we play them.

That will be my legacy forever: "He shouldn't have run the reverse." And I do love the reverse. But my favorite is the sweep. I wouldn't mind if (offensive coordinator) Mark Richt ran that ten times a game.

SUCCESS

The pressure is obvious, because people always expect more when you're successful. But that's okay. It's like growing old. It ain't so bad when you consider the alternative.

It sure makes it difficult (being No. 1), but it comes with the territory. When you're targeted, get ready. The only thing is, we've been in that position before. At least we should learn from it.

—on being a pre-season No. 1

> BOBBY AND I ARE VERY SIMILAR, EXCEPT I LIKE TO HAVE AN OCCASIONAL BEER AND BOBBY GOES TO THE WRONG CHURCH.
>
> *—Joe Paterno, Penn State head football coach*

TELEVISION

Any television show I have or radio show I have, you have to have sponsors. You hear a lot of public complaints from boosters or alumni: "Are (big companies) just buying the university?" Well, somebody has to pay the bills.

Hmmmm. This is one beautiful piece of crystal. (Phil Coale photo)

They'd be pretty good if I could teach the guy to act.
> —referring to the Bobby Bowden television show
> when Burt Reynolds appears as guest

Don't kid yourself that in the top recruits' homes, they don't bring those commercials up. It's an edge for me.

(Boxing) might be the only thing I'd rather watch than football. I'd turn off a football game to watch a good fight.

I had not been that scared since I was fourteen, when I had to give piano recitals. My mind was a blank. I didn't have a clue what to say. I was just standing there thinking, "Bowden, how did you get yourself into this?"
> —on appearing with Burt Reynolds before
> a live studio audience on Evening Shade

Afterward the guy who wrote the script came up to me and said, "You know, that's the best script I never wrote."

—following appearance on Evening Shade

Impersonating a football coach—that's all I've ever done.

—on playing a football coach on television

TEMPTATIONS

Nothing interferes with my (weight) staying down so much as the unexpected good meal—someone lays one out there. I love chicken and dumplings, and I love that old Southern deal of getting a big orange (soda) and putting peanuts in it. And a meal is not nearly complete unless I have a dessert.

That old devil is always out there waiting for another chance. That sneaky guy doesn't give up.

Shoot, I'm a sinner. You're a sinner. We're all sinners. If we acknowledge the truth of the Bible, we know man is born with the seed to sin.

I chew on any kind (of cigar). But to be honest, it's better if they're pretty expensive. The others unravel.

When it comes to chocolate, I'm just like an alcoholic, to be honest. You heard how alcoholics hid their bottle up in the house, I got boxes of candy hid all over the house. When the doctor ever calls me and tells me, "Bowden, you ain't got but four days left," I'm going to eat every bit of it.

I have no prejudices when it comes to food. I will eat anything.

It is kinda one of my ways to be bad.

—on chewing Red Man tobacco

TIME LINE

When I was in Alabama, all I heard was "Beat Auburn." When I was at West Virginia, all I heard was "Beat Pitt." When I got to FSU, their bumper stickers read "Beat Anybody!"

I could think of only two jobs that could have been worse— 1) being elected mayor of Atlanta shortly after Sherman left town or 2) being the general who volunteers to replace George Custer during the last siege at Little Big Horn.
—referring to his accepting the position as FSU's head football coach

It's gonna take longer than I thought.
—after losing his first two games of his first season at FSU, in 1976

When I thought we would win eight, I left out one important factor—attitude. Not that it was bad. It was just that we were not on the same page. And some had lost so many games, they felt they could not win. That had to be changed.

The Book of Bowden

You could say the FSU program started growing some whiskers in 1979 and 1980, and it started shaving every day in 1981.

If any crazy guy out there is talking 11-0 because we're excited around here, he'd better wise up.

−1976

She wasn't pretty, but she was a win. A lot of it on offense has to do with the play calling, and I'm responsible for a lot of that junk we called.

—on the Seminoles beating Virginia Tech, 17-10, in 1979

I had a good alibi ready. Then those crazy guys go out and win the game.

—on beating Cincinnati in 1979

Did we win or lose this? It's hard to believe we won the doggone game. Every time I looked up, someone else was winning it. I guess it was just our time.

–after beating Nebraska in the 1993 Orange Bowl

It was a very wasted drench. It was extremely cold, and then we had to win it again.

–when players doused Bowden with ice near the end of the 1994 Orange Bowl game

TRADITION

I want to be the head coach at Florida State from now on because we're gonna build tradition into this program just like they've done at other tradition football teams. I love the fans, the state of Florida, and the enthusiasm that everyone has around here. Hopefully, this thing is gonna last forever.

–in November 1979 before signing a new contract

The Book of Bowden

> I'VE USED THINGS IN MY LIFE THAT (COACH BOWDEN) TAUGHT ME IN THE ONE YEAR I HAD WITH HIM. THINGS I'LL TRY TO TEACH MY CHILDREN.
>
> —*Jimmy Black, Bowden's first quarterback at FSU, 1976*

VALUES

I believe in a three-team system, offense, defense—and academics. I don't say that to be funny. When a boy comes to school and doesn't want academics, you're in trouble.

Football ain't life-or-death . . . I've always tried to impress on my players that they should know the difference between what's important in life and what's unimportant, and to keep their priorities straight. Like I've said thousands of times, football is important to me, but it's not the most important thing. My faith, my salvation, is what is important.

—reflecting on senior offensive tackle Pablo Lopez's death in 1986

My family is more important than football, and my religion is more important than either one.

The entire clan of Bobby and Ann Bowden hit the beach. Postcard perfect, huh? (Catherine L. Strauss, photographer)

> I THINK WHEN ALL IS SAID AND DONE, HE'LL BE RANKED UP THERE WITH BEAR BRYANT AS ONE OF THE GREATEST COACHES EVER.
>
> –Brad Johnson, FSU quarterback 1991

WINNING

Now here's the part that must seem so contradictory. I feel like I've got to risk losing to keep on winning. There's just no way around it. To win consistently, you've got to put yourself in a position where you're liable to lose.

The winning doesn't feel as good as the losing does bad.

One thing. One thing won this game, heart.

–*after a comeback victory against Virginia in 1995*

The crown fits better when you're way ahead.

–*referring to the Homecoming chief and princess being crowned at halftime*

I am not happy with moral victories. Those things are forgotten.

WINNING TRAITS

It's amazing. Some of the greatest characteristics of being a winning football player are the same ones it's true to be a good man, to be a religious man, to be—in my case—a Christian man.

Let me tell you what it takes to make a winning player—I got to have discipline, I got to have obedience, I got to have boys who love each other and will fight for each other. I got to have boys that are loyal, I got to have boys that are enthusiastic. I got to have boys who will sacrifice, I got to have boys who will train their bodies, I got to have boys who have courage, I got to have boys who have resolution.

The X's and the O's are just not a big part of football; it's there—you got to have a structured way of running a play and a defense—but, boy, it gets down to heart, it gets down to soul, it gets down to enthusiasm. It gets down to desire, it gets down to attitude, and all those things have to come from inside of a guy, you know.

It used to be years ago, when I first started playing football, you didn't talk about love and football in the same (sentence). How could you play football and love? I'll tell you how: We talk about teams having the chemistry: "Man, this ball club had good chemistry." I think what that means, you got a bunch of boys that love and care for each other, you see when somebody loves somebody, they'll fight for them, when somebody loves somebody, they'll defend them, when somebody loves somebody, they're not gonna let somebody hurt that person, and that's a big thing in football.

I tell our players everything starts mentally, in other words, the body doesn't do anything that the mind doesn't tell it to do. If I want this body to perform, my mind has got to tell it what to do.

The Bible tells us, "And the peace of God, which surpasses all understanding, will guard your hearts and minds through Christ Jesus." (Philippians 4:7) When you have the God of love in your heart and mind, you certainly can't have a lousy life.

I tell my players, "If I have your faith, trust, and commitment, then we're gonna win a heckuva lot of games. I think God is looking for the same ingredients in each of us: faith, trust, and commitment."

Where do you get the spirit and desire to excel athletically? From only one place—from God. Only He can motivate you to be the best you can be.

> HE'S GOT A RELATIONSHIP WITH HIS PLAYERS THAT'S HARD TO GET. HE KEEPS CHANGING WITH THE TIMES, AND THAT'S A WONDERFUL TRAIT TO HAVE. HE CAN HANDLE AND MOTIVATE THE PLAYERS IN THE NINETIES JUST AS HE DID IN THE FIFTIES.
>
> —Lee Corso, ESPN analyst, FSU quarterback 1953–1956

YOUTH

Trust is the absolute last thing a lot of kids are willing to invest these days. For many of the ones we see, there's nothing in their experience that suggests much of a payoff in trusting somebody else. The lessons they come to school with are lessons of the street: Get the other guy before he gets you. Never turn your back. Don't depend on anybody.

There are just too many diversions, too many other outlets for their energies. It's awfully hard for today's young people—and some older people—to keep their minds on a higher goal. It's so easy for them to get off track.

> THE ONLY REGRET I HAVE IS THAT I NEVER HAD A CHANCE TO PLAY FOR BOBBY BOWDEN.
>
> *–Burt Reynolds*

Two legends with a common passion for FSU football—Burt Reynolds and Bobby Bowden. (Phil Coale photo)

www.ingramcontent.com/pod-product-compliance
Lightning Source LLC
Chambersburg PA
CBHW051414070526
44584CB00023B/3424